Improve Yc

Guide to Exercises and Techniques for Boosting Your IQ
So That You Can Learn Better, Maintain Focus Longer
and Be More Successful in General

By Nathan Weaver

Contents

Thank you for buying this book and I hope that you will find it useful. If you will want to share your thoughts on this book, you can do so by leaving a review on the Amazon page, it helps me out a lot.

Chapter 1: The Importance of Reading

Reading enhances brain functionality and has a direct connection with increased IQs. Kids who read effectively have much better odds of succeeding in school, and are typically in the gifted classes. How do you get kids to wish to read? You do that by reading to them.

Begin reading to your kids early and daily. Demonstrate to them how wonderful books could be in order to make them think that within every cover is a wonderful world. If your kid delights in a specific story, read it once again. There's nothing bad in reading the identical story again, as a matter of fact, it strengthens the reality that reading should be a habit.

Read at the identical time(s) daily. Right prior to bed is an exceptional time since it eliminates 2 birds with one stone. It assists in enhancing their visualization and creativity abilities and makes them eagerly anticipate bed.

What books are ideal to improve IQ? The classics such as Dr. Seuss aid by utilizing poetry. Rhymes promote brain activity and promote memorization.

Another way to get kids into reading is to enable them to choose the books. All reading is reading. Even if you prefer that they read Shakespeare at 8, that does not suggest that it is any better for them than the most recent Batman comic. The aim is not to push them; it is to impart in them a love of books and reading. Motivate them to read. Do not turn them off by pushing them to do it, or requiring them to read something they do not take pleasure in. You might enjoy the adventures of Elizabeth Bennet to Bruce Wayne, however, your kid might not.

Much of the book shops have fantastic kids' sections, and you may discover that your kid is going to go through lots of books while there. They normally have playrooms and games to ensure that children spend more time there (and it motivates the parents to search for more books). Permit your kid to stroll the aisles, opening and reading a couple of pages up until he/she picks just the ideal book. This is going to get them thrilled about reading.

As they are young, get things going by helping them by reading to them yourself. One sentence at once. Slowly develop their vocabulary and capabilities. Eventually, they are going to be doing the reading, and you are going to be doing the listening. Even after your kid is reading on his/her own, continue sticking to the schedule. Chapter books with their mini-cliff hangers are one manner of tricking your kid into wishing to learn more. More notably, chapter books push them to read more and more complex content that develops the brain's critical thinking capabilities, which consequently, enhances their IQ

Chapter 2: Exercising Your Brain

Everybody wishes to know how to improve their IQ. Many researchers think that you can raise your IQ in between 10 and 20 points by means of "exercising" the brain. Here is an activity list that you can tackle to assist with enhancing your mental capacity in order to improve your IQ.

1. First off, and this one is practically a given, participate in puzzles and other brain activities such as sudoku.

2. Block one (or more) of the senses, and after that, take part in home cleaning activities. This pushes the brain to rewire itself.

3. On that identical note, Support ambidexterity, and ambidextrous habits. For instance, the non-dominant hand for dominant hand activities such as brushing your teeth or writing.

4. Engage your brain in imaginative activities such as music, art, or writing.

5. Discover another usage for every little thing in your home. For instance, what additional things could you utilize a nail file for?

6. Discover the subtleties of tasting the wine; this forces the brain to use other senses.

7. Discover how to juggle.

8. Take on an extreme sport such as rock climbing or skateboarding.

9. Go to comedy shows. Laugh. Have a good time.

10. Play more. Imaginative activities activate the brain, so do not hesitate to play with dolls or action figures with your kids.

11. Obtain more sleep. The brain requires it to dream and restore itself.

12. Get rid of the calculator and do basic arithmetic yourself.

13. Ejoy classical music.

14. Discover something brand-new daily.

15. Try chess.

16. Play video games (do not cheer too much for this one).

17. Keep a diary or journal.

18. Eat healthy. Stay clear of sugars; include more anti-oxidants into your eating plan.

19. Exercise is shown to energize the brain.

20. Discover a brand-new language.

21. Discover how to speed read.

22. Go through books.

23. Shut off the TV and opt for a walk.

24. Consume a great deal of water.

25. Sign up with a debating club.

These are a few of the important things you may do to test your brain. Like a professional athlete modifying the workout program, you need to modify how you think and how you do things. Do not allow the gray matter waste away. Come up with your own list of activities which are going to make you look at life as a puzzle, and you are on your path to truly activating that what you were born with.

Chapter 3: Increasing Your IQ via Exercise

The brain is a muscle, and just like every other muscle, it requires the following: oxygen, nutrients, and exercise. Here are certain valuable pointers for improving your IQ that might amaze you.

Constantly consume an excellent breakfast. The brain utilizes glucose as its main source of energy, so consuming breakfast is going to enhance concentration, problem-solving, memory, mood, and general psychological efficiency. Without fuel, no engine can do its thing. Ensure that you are consuming Omega 3s, folic acid, iron, and supplying it with oxygen and hydration. Keep in mind: stay away from the corn syrup and cut down on carbs and sugars. Insulin rushing into the bloodstream to counteract the rush of sugars squanders energy and makes you drowsy and sluggish, less capable to think.

Ensure to obtain your supply of anti-oxidants. Anti-oxidants shield all the cells of the body, as well as those in the brain. Superfoods consist of the highest levels of anti-oxidants, like: blueberries, blackberries, acai berries, garlic, plums, spinach, cranberries, raspberries, and strawberries.

Go out and move. Motion is an essential part of growth and learning. Sports help with critical thinking abilities, and they raise mood and flood the brain with chemicals such as adrenalin and serotonin. You can combat memory loss, hone the intelligence, and function at peak by raising your heart rate. Scientific proof demonstrates that aerobic exercise tweaks the brain for so it can perform at its peak.

Neuropsychologists think that meditation and practices like yoga or prayer can, in fact, change brain structure. MRI scans of Franciscan and Tibetan monks while encountering diversions demonstrated that long-term meditators have a higher resistance to diversion and much better capability to solve problems throughout diversions as opposed to individuals who do not practice this.

Play! Games of any type activate the brain and push it into overdrive. Be it hide and seek, kickball, or softball, playing sports assists with establishing critical thinking abilities.

Chapter 4: Use Puzzles

The human brain is an amazing instrument. The processes of the human brain have actually undergone a study after rigorous research study by the world's biggest minds, and still, we understand fairly little about how it functions. Nevertheless, there is one truth that all professionals can agree upon, which is that the human brain gains from exercise just as your muscles do. As a matter of fact, your brain benefits from exercising, and it additionally flourishes due to it. Which exercises does your brain take pleasure in? Deductive reasoning, creativity, and puzzle-solving are what provide your brain with a boost, along with enhancing your fluid intelligence.

There are 2 kinds of intelligence: fluid and crystallized. Crystallized intelligence is when your brain relies on the understanding of existing capabilities to fix an issue, IE, your memory. Something worked one time previously, so it is going to work once again. Fluid intelligence depends on your brain's capability to evaluate and comprehend the relationships and cases in between numerous ideas or artifacts when dealing with issues. Fluid intelligence is independent of previous knowledge, experience or capability. As IQ is your capability to get to know "new" things, by training your brain on how to learn those new things, IE exercising, you are improving your IQ.

Puzzles such as Sudoku and games such as chess can boost your mental age by as much as 14 years and ward off the beginning of illnesses such as Alzheimer's. Solving a Rubik's cube could additionally assist in boosting the cognitive element of your IQ. The puzzle itself is among the most misspelled English words. Rubik's Cube was created in the '70s by a Hungarian architect.

It is stated to be the most among the most prominent toys on the planet! It additionally serves to promote grey matter. If you can't discover one in your neighborhood toy shop, then you're bound to know a person who has actually one kept away in a dark deep box in their attic or tossed behind the couch in a moment of hefty disappointment. If not, get one at your neighborhood goodwill shop for cents and get shuffling and activating the grey matter.

Finally, you can place yourself more in the present with mindfulness techniques, and you are going to provide yourself with more mental capacity. These distinct exercises place you in a state of awareness and permit you to let go of interruptions. If done frequently, these exercises allow you to think more plainly and assist you to focus. The most standard mindfulness exercise starts with just unwinding and breathing deeply. Shut your eyes and take notice of your breathing. After some time, shift your focus to your body, a single part at a time, observing any feelings or anything you could recognize. After a couple of minutes of attention on your body, begin listening to the sounds of the area, without criticizing or judging. Simply listen. Your brain, similarly to a muscle, requires time to recuperate.

Chapter 5: The Mozart Effect

The Mozart Effect is a theory based upon outcomes from a research that demonstrated that students who listened to Mozart prior to a spatial reasoning test had a boost of as much as 9 points in their IQ. Even though the boost was just for a brief time period (10 to 15 minutes), it did demonstrate improvement. The term was initially coined by Alfred A. Tomatis. He utilized the music as a listening stimulus to attempt to negate particular effects stemming from mental illness. It was then made popular in 1994 in the New York Times.

The science behind the effect is really rather straightforward. The scientists think that intelligence was enhanced due to the fact that the brain and the ear are 2 distinct entities but join forces to produce the listening experience. When an acoustic wave strikes the ear, it is then sent out by means of electric impulses to the brain for processing. Hearing Mozart or any peaceful music appears to warm up the pathways and synapses within the brain.

This makes it possible for the information to be processed properly and more effectively, rendering it feasible to remember and to use that information better.

Even though many individuals think that listening to Mozart makes you more clever, this is not correct. The impacts of the music are more associated with spatial-temporal activities, including temporal ordering and mental imagery and not intelligence. Nevertheless, increasing those qualities boosts your capability to take in information. The ideal outcomes have actually appeared in kids. Some state it's due to the fact that the brain is still establishing and makes it possible for such an activity in the brain to carry on.

Some researchers think that the sole connection this research has anything to do with is the arousal and mood that the music places you in. Even with their thinking, it just confirms that the theory to have credibility. Music impacts various individuals in various manners. The research has actually been used in other fields too. Some latest tests on epileptic individuals have actually demonstrated a decline in epileptiform activity. Much research study is being put into the psychoacoustic field for several conditions and for lots of developments of the human brain. Developments in this field might result in some significant innovations in the comprehension of how the mind operates and how we are able to make it work for us.

Chapter 6: Fundamentals of Increasing Your IQ

How many times have we wished to be more intelligent? Pass an advanced physics course? It's constantly that one issue, the IQ, that gets us in trouble. IQ means Intelligence Quotient and is utilized to assess the intelligence of a person via screening. The typical IQ is between 84 and 113, the low range is 26-41 (that shows a serious psychological impairment), and anything over 174 is taken into consideration as "Exceptionally Blessed." Since the introduction of IQ screening, individuals all over have actually been attempting to boost their IQ.

There are plenty of methods to boost your IQ. Plenty of programs are offered online, however, are they worth it? A more typical manner in which you can boost your IQ is via "mental exercises," a kind of workout for the grey matter. Games produced the Nintendo DS like Brain Age I and II, and Big Brain Academy appear to be made with brain exercising in mind. Performing mind teaser puzzles and things such as Sudoku and even crosswords can assist in keeping your mind in shape, and there's an included benefit: keeping Alzheimer's at bay!

A couple of pointers:

1. Don't watch TV as much

2. Get a good night's sleep

3. Work out!

They might seem straightforward, however, keeping the remainder of your body fit helps your brain out quite well. Another means to assist with your IQ may be to simply take a seat and pop some Mozart music. It's a short-term effect, however, in case you find yourself requiring some assistance prior to a test, have a go at 2 Pianos in D Major, K. 448, or any other track by the popular artist. Consuming much healthier foods additionally assists.

A number of the sites or things I have actually discovered on my journey of IQ increase, are typically unproven and do not generally work. In this facet, please know what you may be entering into if you try to buy an online program. The Web is swarming with cons, and you do not need to be a genius to discover which ones are. My slogan is, "take care if they ask for cash!" The ideal programs I customize around myself, and helpful ideas and techniques (and a couple of Nintendo DS games) to produce my own specifically created program for raising my IQ!

Chapter 7: How to Learn Better

Before you begin cramming for the following midterm, take a couple of minutes and consider how you are tackling learning the criteria. Numerous people believe that learning is learning, which it is, however, there are a number of things you may do to assist you with taking in the knowledge much more. One easy thing to do is to be in a relaxing, calm location when studying. Chaotic areas add to messy thinking. Take a while to arrange a location in which you are comfy.

Unwinding is a significant key in having the ability to process the information effectively. Do whatever you have to do to be comfy. Light a couple of candles, take a couple of deep breaths, or stretch. Additionally, you ought to consider some time out, so you are not going to be troubled.

Another thing that is going to assist a lot is practicing meditation prior to a study session. Meditation is commonly utilized in several contexts. It has actually been utilized all throughout history in non-religious and religious customs in attempting to get to a high level of awareness or enlightenment. Meditation is a procedure of concentrating the mind on a single item without any diversion. It is additionally referred to as a state of awareness when there are no dispersed thoughts or diverse patterns.

In regards to utilizing it to learn, it is a really helpful tool. Think of it such as this, your brain resembles a muscle and has to be warmed up and stretched prior to appropriately operate at its max capacity. Practicing meditation enables you to soothe the brain and clear it of thoughts. This renders it feasible to think about something with a lot more effectiveness and precision. The brain is going to then have the ability to process and ingest the information, and it's as easy as simply taking a seat, shutting your eyes, and emptying your head.

Ever think to yourself, "Wow, I truly am great at this." Well, you ought to more frequently if you do not. Simply trusting in yourself boosts your potential to learn more effectively. The positive idea is, without a doubt, among the simplest methods to assist you in learning. Additionally, having an excellent mindset about wishing to learn is required.

If you do not wish to learn, then you will have a difficult time doing anything. The positive thoughts and mindsets are going to assist you with boosting your learning capacity, and they are going to additionally set you up for a great life.

Chapter 8: Herbs for IQ

The next supplements and herbs have actually been shown to help with increasing brain activity and increasing your IQ.

1. Gingko Biloba extracts or leaves are recognized for boosting the blood circulation to the brain. You can, in fact, consume the leaves (the trees are discovered in plenty of parks), or purchase supplements.

2. Phosphatidyl Serine (PS) is a supplement which has actually been researched in clinical trials and has actually demonstrated proof of boosting the learning rate and lucidity in those taking it. It obviously triggers cell-to-cell interaction, enhances special receptor performance, and readies cells for activity.

3. Vinpocetine, an extract obtained from alkaloids discovered in the Periwinkle plant, is a cerebral vasodilator, indicating that it boosts blood

There are lots of "brain foods" available that you can consume, a number of which include the supplements pointed out. Wheatgrass and other greens are understood to be helpful for the whole body. Simply make certain to eat properly, stay clear of sugars, and drink a great deal of water, and your brain is going to be happy.

Chapter 9: Importance of Concentration

Have you ever been tackling something and simply feel mentally drained? Ending up being aggravated due to the fact that you simply can not think effectively is common for all people. A couple of individuals understand, though, that it's much like going for a run. When you reach the point of fatigue, pushing yourself a bit more permits you to develop your muscles and boost endurance. Well, your brain is precisely like that. The following time you get to that fatigue point when thinking, simply push yourself a little more. Pushing yourself past your capability is going to just help your brain.

Another simple method to focus much better is just doing one thing at a time. Although, as people, we can multitask, commit your attention to one subject rather than several things. It might appear too easy to be helpful, however, it actually is very important when it comes to being able to focus much better. The worst obstacle to your focus is procrastination. Delaying tasks or thinking that you are going to do them later on impacts the work quality which is going to get done.

Tasks take longer to accomplish when you are not mentally there. There are a number of methods around procrastination; however, among the easiest is a series of 3 questions to ask yourself. The initial question is, do I need to do this? Then ask yourself, do I want it completed, so I don't have to think about it? Lastly, ask is it going to be less troublesome later on? After asking these questions, you are going to discover that the easy questions bring you to conclude that this issue is not disappearing up until you deal with it.

Studying in an excellent area when attempting to focus is a necessity for good learning. If you are stuck in an area loaded with diversions, it appears apparent that it is going to be additionally difficult to get anything accomplished. Put in the time to discover a location where you could be without diversions. Additionally, plan some time throughout your day to, in fact, accomplish what you have to. Do not only attempt to squeeze in some studying when it is practical. It is going to place you under more tension, and it is not going to allow for the absorption of the material in an excellent way. Ensure you are additionally in an excellent state of mind. Keeping your brain delighted is going to keep you delighted when you recognize just how much more you are taking in.

Chapter 10: How to Use Your Increased IQ

Apparently, the IQ test determines how smart you are as opposed to the remainder of the population. Alfred Binet, of France, pioneered the initial IQ test. He wished to distinguish between "regular" kids and those who were having a hard time. An American man called Lewis Terman reworked the test to what we understand today as the "Stanford-Binet" IQ test, which is questionable for the primary reason that intelligence depends mainly on aspects like environment, community, childhood, and most notably, genes.

A number of history's smartest individuals didn't rank exceptionally high on IQ tests. The IQ scoring system is typically misinterpreted. 90-110 is regularly taken into consideration as "ordinary," Whereas 130 or over is incredibly smart, and around just 2% of the population attains this rating.

Nevertheless, lots of research studies have actually demonstrated ways to boost your mental capacity. Frances Rauscher, a psychologist, discovered that enjoying Baroque music appeared to enhance brainpower. Kids who acquire music lessons score better on IQ tests, too.

Eating healthy appears to play an essential role, also. Essential fats are important to our brain function. Eicosapentaenoic acid, or EPA, is discovered in fish oil. Have you ever noticed how there was a boost in pregnant ladies taking fish oil supplements? This is why. Naturally, consuming a well-balanced diet plan that has fresh fruits and veggies, along with being hydrated, is also important. Exercise is additionally a crucial element in preserving brain function.

Mental activities like reading, quizzes, and puzzles maintain your brain in top shape. These "mental exercises" maintain your capability to process information, much as exercising in the gym keeps physical stamina. Research studies have actually demonstrated these activities can boost IQ ratings by approximately 8%.

Research studies demonstrate that neural wires send electrical messages within the brain. Each nerve cell covered with a fatty myelin layer, that insulates and enables the messages to travel at optimum speed. The healthier the myelin, the greater the IQ. Sadly, lots of things can disrupt this function. A few of the most notorious perpetrators of brain dysfunction are alcohol and drugs.

Positive thinking is a reasonably brand-new advancement relating physical health and psychology. In case you are giving yourself negative messages, more than likely, you are going to act upon these negative messages. Lots of research studies have actually confirmed that anxiety can impact physical health, especially the heart. There is no question that this would additionally impact the brain.

Chapter 11: Boosting Mental Capacity

Mental capacity is your capability to plan, reason, and solve problems, use language, and learn. This is simply one part of your overall intelligence. Similar to the physical body, your brain could be trained like a muscle, making it more powerful. One manner in which you can enhance the brain is by placing yourself simply outside your comfort zone. Placing yourself and your brain in various types of settings that are different enables your brain to strain a bit and grow.

There are a couple of things you may do to aid this procedure in daily life. When you're hungry, have a go at some food you have not actually tried out yet. Simply a little tweak in your day can make a big change. The list of things you may do is limitless and differs with everyone. That is what makes the human brain one the most incredible things ever. All people are physically and genetically identical, however, every person's brain is distinct.

There are a few other things you may do in case you feel you have actually struck a wall, such as returning to school and finding out how to play an instrument or just doing something that activates your brain. Doing things that you delight in is a substantial advantage for apparent reasons. When doing an activity you delight in, your brain gets a reward, and you grow psychologically from that. A poor influence would be watching TV, considering that watching it does not utilize your capability, and it does not allow you to gain back mental energy. In case you are about to watch TV, watch something informative or something that is going to make you think. Utilize the brain rather than simply allowing it to vegetate.

As all of us grow older, we have a tendency to forget our minds. It gets more difficult to maintain the brain active as we get older because of an absence of social stimulants or simple laziness. All is not lost, however. There are methods for maintaining the sharpness of the mind. Among the simplest methods out there are crossword puzzles. Puzzles of any sort are great for your psychological health. In case you are more daring and believe that you can take a challenge, try juggling. This boosts your psychological acuity and hand-eye coordination.

Chapter 12: Advantages of Working Out and Sleeping

I'm certain we have actually all met that one individual who simply happens to score more than everybody on their tests, and simply appears to constantly get greater grades than the rest. We've all had our times of envy for the individual who has a greater IQ than everybody else, and we question, how do they do this? There are numerous aspects that fall into your IQ and the various things that are able to boost or harm your IQ. As a matter of fact, a few of these could be performed in your own home, for free!

Stress no more! An easy method to boost your IQ would be to attempt to work out. It's a thing that everybody may do in his/her own home for only a couple of minutes every day. There are numerous things that can aid your IQ, however, working out is a fantastic method to begin, and is a thing that could be adapted to fit the level of any specific individual that would wish to include it to their everyday schedule. Regardless of whether you are a beginner or a fitness instructor, working out can assist in boosting your IQ and can additionally open your mind to additional learning.

The implementation of exercise could be viewed as a means of awakening your mind. It is going to it awaken your mind, and it can additionally offer your body more energy to carry on with the day, whereas you would generally be exhausted. This can vary from taking a slight jog to walking in the morning to rigorous cardio workouts in your home or at the fitness center. Any type of exercise could work as a way to boost your IQ.

Another simple method to boost your IQ would be to go to sleep on a routine basis every night. As we grow older, our everyday schedule changes, and our routines differ on a daily basis. Because of these adjustments, we are sleep deprived, and we wind up depriving our bodies of its rest. Well, along with cheating our bodies, we really are denying our minds of what it requires. Along with the amount of rest, quality is necessary too. If you sleep for 8 hours yet are uneasy for 5, then it's much like sleeping for 3 hours. For this to be helpful, your sleep quality is extremely crucial.

Chapter 13: What is the Brain About?

The brain is the supercomputer of the body. Human brains are very complicated. They are composed of countless nerve cells and as much as 10 000 synaptic connections. Think about your brain as a large muscle that manages practically every little thing within your body. Keeping it in top condition is a top priority in life. The brain manages all the significant systems of the body. The growth of the brain is necessary in order to be more intelligent and more capable of managing it. Training it much like you would train your body plays a significant role in the elevation of your intelligence. Eating correctly, looking after your body, and continually training are what you need to do to remain smart.

Similar to the body, your brain has to be exercised daily to remain in shape. You additionally have to maintain your body in good shape as they are identical. Lifting weights, taking walks, and eating correctly are all possible ways of improving your intelligence. In case you have no energy, your brain is not going to operate correctly. Ever attempted doing homework incredibly late during the night. It is tough, isn't it? Merely obtaining a full night's rest is going to boost your capabilities. Sleep deprivation has a significant part in whether your brain is going to be working properly.

Another easy and pleasurable way to assist with the procedure of brain training is eating well. There are 3 essential neurotransmitters in the brain, and they are Dopamine, Acetylcholine, and Serotonin. Acetylcholine is in charge of memory, concentration, and focus. A couple of foods you can consume to enhance this are egg yolks, meat, peanuts, fish, dairy products, liver, and veggies. Dopamine is in charge of smart learning. The easiest manner in which you can increase your levels of dopamine with food is to consume any source of protein. Serotonin is in charge of memory and learning. Carbs include the building blocks for the serotonin. Pasta, bread, cereals, potatoes, and starchy veggies are all excellent to enhance your serotonin levels.

An excellent way to maintain your brain fit is to utilize it. As easy as it sounds, lots of people do not do this correctly. Rather than dreaming or considering that useless idea, take that energy and concentrate it on another thing. Doing something you delight in additionally assists with this procedure. The brain is among the most complicated organs in the body. It's simple to look after it if you wish to put the time in.

Chapter 14: How to Remember More

For most people, attempting to remember the countless things taught to us in school is nearly hopeless. The information retention could be broken down into 3 phases. If you practice and comply with a couple of easy actions, you can enhance your retention capabilities.

The initial phase in the remembering procedure is acquisition. Where did you learn this, or what event occurred? It is vital in the initial phase to pay extremely careful attention to what is being taught. The next phase of retention is the combination stage. This is when the information or memory is sent to long term memory for storage. At this moment in time, the more you center your focus on the information, the simpler it is going to be to extract it afterwards. It is additionally handy to connect the memory to an older memory as it is going to be simpler to get it back.

The third and last phase is the retrieval procedure. This is when you, in fact, have to get the information out and utilize it. The more you consider that particular though prior to attempting to obtain it, the simpler it is going to be to, in fact, recall it in the future. In case you are still having difficulty attempting to recover a particular memory, it assists if you are in the identical location where you learned what you are attempting to recall. This is simply one easy method to assist with enhancing your memory, and there are numerous other methods.

There are additionally a couple of approaches you ought to take while attempting to hold on to knowledge. As opposed to common belief, focusing actually does assist a lot. For something to be stored effectively in your brain, you need to really learn what it is. Additionally, individuals are extremely distinct in all kinds of manners, particularly in the manner in which we learn. Much of us learn in a specific manner. It is advised to determine how you learn most effectively and utilize that to your benefit. When diving into really difficult studies, it is ideal to attempt to learn the essentials of it, and then associate the more complicated concepts with the essentials, as it is going to enable much better understanding and retention. Taking brand-new information and connecting it to older information is a good technique when attempting to recall a great deal of information.

Much like anything concerning your body, being healthy is important. Eating well and getting a lot of exercise play a huge part in your capability to remember. Getting a lot of rest and staying clear of difficult circumstances is also recommended.

Chapter 15: Be Smart By Remaining Active

Intelligence is certainly subjective. Everybody wishes to be clever. However, how to tackle it in the best manner? Here are certain ideas you can utilize to assist with increasing your own intelligence.

Adventure

Adrenaline can provide you with a momentary boost in your intelligence. Routine exposure can be good for your long-term I.Q., along with boosting your capability to think clearly under pressure. Bungee jumping, skateboarding, and mountain climbing are all intense sports that need fast thinking. Simply take a look at Tony Hawk, who claims to have an I.Q of 144.

Stay Clear Of Repetition

Repetitive activities dull the mind. Activities such as assembly line work or Farmville need minimal thought, and your mind goes into a state of auto-pilot for hours at a time. When challenged with a brand-new scenario that needs critical thinking, your mind needs to get rid of the fog of auto-pilot. The longer one takes part in meaningless repetitive activity the more difficult it ends up being to get rid of that fog later on

Diet plan

Set down that Big Mac. It is actually numbing you down. Fast food doesn't just clog your arteries, it also blocks your brain's capability to think. Your eating plan adds to mindset just as much as your physical state. Have a go at raw or brown sugar instead of bleached white sugar. Have some orange juice rather than soda. Consume more salad. Unhealthy diets result in bad thinking, so do not sell yourself short when picking what to eat. In case you eat properly, you are going to think properly.

Hypnosis

There are a lot of hypnosis programs you could download or see on YouTube to boost your speed of reading, perception memory, and so on. In the convenience and security of your own home, you can utilize these hypnosis programs to enhance your thinking procedure. It is not a magic bullet as much as it is a tool such as every other someone can utilize, and the more you utilize it, the better your outcomes are going to be.

Utilize the Web

On the internet, you can discover sites that are going to teach you brand-new languages, offer binaural beats, and provide philosophical discourse, and a lot more. Use it as much as you can. And if you only desire the question answered for you, the Web may do that as well. The point is that there are a lot of folks the web happy to supply pointers and tools to assist for minimal to no cost, it's simply stupid not to utilize it.

This is merely the short list. There are a lot more things you may do to push your noggin in the appropriate direction. If you begin with these little actions initially, then you ought to be more than capable of taking the larger steps by yourself. And do not rush it. Excellent minds are not created overnight. It takes some time. One sky diving lesson and a salad is not going to turn you into Albert Einstein. Nevertheless, if you keep at it, you are going to become as clever as you wish to be.

Chapter 16: More Ways to Boost your IQ

Your IQ stands for your intelligence quotient and is what is utilized to determine how clever you are, or your intelligence level. Growing up, all of us had experiences wherein we wished to increase our IQ level, or perhaps now, we wish to boost our mental capacity. Specialists have actually studied and investigated this to discover manners in which this could be accomplished. There are numerous manners in which this could be done, and you can do a lot in the comfort of your own home by making easy tweaks to your everyday or weekly schedule. These couple of tweaks might affect your IQ more than you might know.

One method for boosting your IQ would be to attempt meditation. To some people, this might appear insane due to the fact that it's not something that everybody does, or that lots of people are even ready to attempt to put into their day-to-day schedules. Nevertheless, if carried out correctly, meditation might increase your IQ, and might most likely do good things for your brainpower.

Meditation can assist due to the fact that it affects how you breathe and your breathing level. If we think about our everyday lives, how many times do we make an effort to take deep, long breaths every day? We most likely do not do this typically or perhaps whatsoever. However, deep breathing can affect our IQ a lot. By incorporating deep breathing, it could make us more unwinded, which can open and unwind our minds too and can even assist us in discharging tension. This could be done for merely a couple of minutes a day. It's something little that could lead to huge enhancements and does not even need a great deal of time.

Another method of boosting your IQ would be writing. These days, due to technology, a lot of us do not put in the time to write, due to every little thing that's available that makes us think that we don't need to write. There are numerous other methods of interaction that leads to many individuals not wishing to write. Nevertheless, this can assist us by utilizing elements of our brain that we hardly ever utilize regularly. Instead of sending somebody an email, attempt to write them a letter by hand which can boost your IQ really quickly in a short time. This is one fast method to boost your IQ in your home.

Chapter 17: Increasing Your Kid's IQ

Behavioral researchers are the initial ones to say to you that your IQ is not fixed. You can enhance it by eating well, exercising, and inducing brain activity. This summer season, aim to increase your kid's IQ by working with them on enjoyable and purposeful activities.

Kids who read effectively have a tendency to write effectively, and writing effectively, results in reading well. This effective mix of writing and reading offers kids an increase in their mental capacity. Writing needs creativity, reflection, and problem-solving abilities. Have your kid keep a summer season journal or perhaps a creative writing note pad. When a kid assesses their everyday experiences, they boost both their intelligence and psychological quotient. When writing, they are improving problem-solving abilities! Scrapbooking is a vibrant alternative to the common journal and additionally aids with fine motor skills.

Sports and outside activities assist your kids in remaining healthy, and they additionally increase mental capacity. Outside play assists in increasing their aerobic levels (which promotes the brain), and employs critical thinking abilities. Furthermore, the imagination that's associated with make-believe games can push their brains to think in a way that improves complicated problem-solving abilities. Outside play (in contrast to indoor), in fact, decreases stress levels in kids. This summer season sends the children outside. Take them on camping or hikes, construct a treehouse together, register them for swim lessons, or perhaps send them to a camp. Children have to be outside, and most children today are regretfully lacking in the kinds of vitamins supplied by sunlight. Whether they like it or not, they have to play outdoors.

Reading is essential. Kids who read throughout their summer season break perform much better in school when they come back in the fall. It matters not what they read, they have to read. Research studies demonstrate that when your kid reads for enjoyment, he/she is going to do better in school than those children who are pushed to read. Take your kid to the library and allow them to select any book they want. All reading benefits them. Make reading enjoyable by establishing a hammock in the yard or enabling them to take the book to their outside forts.

Chapter 18: 10 Easy Ways to Boost IQ

For several years, the typical belief was that an individual's IQ was static, mostly dependant upon somebody's genes. While genes are very important, numerous researchers are discovering that there are strategies that can increase IQ. Here are 10 methods for accomplishing that.

1. Breathing deeper is going to boost the oxygen to your brain, and this is going to assist with boosting brain function. For finest outcomes, inhale through the nose to obtain additional oxygen.

2. Take pauses and breaks. Take pauses an breaks after twenty minutes or half an hour. Simply a brief break is going to provide you time and space to soak in what you learn.

3. Spruce up your diet plan. Keep away from simple carbs and sugars. Sugars and carbs make focus and psychological tasks harder. Boosting anti-oxidants

can assist to shield cells, and this consists of brain cells.

4. Exercise. There are certain research studies that have actually found that boosting the heart rate and breaking a sweat can raise moods, battle loss of memory, and hone the intelligence.

5. Utilize downtime carefully. What do you do while being in a rush-hour or waiting in a line? Utilize this time well and work out the brain. Listen to audiobooks in the vehicle or solve puzzles while you are in line,

6. Journal. There are scientists who have actually studied the practices of 300 individuals who were looked at as geniuses. They discovered that they all had a routine of journaling their experiences and ideas. Thomas Edison, as a matter of fact, recorded his ideas in numerous journals during his life.

7. Read and learn. When we learn, we open brand-new neural pathways. More intelligent individuals are those who have several neural pathways with

numerous connections. Reading more is going to make learning easier. 8. Enjoy games and puzzles. Video games can actually assist with honing your mind. These games push your brain to work rapidly and tactically. Puzzles have a tendency to assist with sharpening the mind in order to come up with great breakthroughs.

9. Have breakfast. Consuming breakfast has actually been demonstrated to enhance focus and psychological efficiency. Glucose is the main energy source for the brain. Breakfast is the initial opportunity your brain has to recharge after 8 hours of sleep.

10. Make use of the morning. It has actually been demonstrated that the brain works optimally the early morning. Knowing that, do as much as you are able to prior to midday.

I hope that you enjoyed reading through this book and that you have found it useful. If you want to share your thoughts on this book, you can do so by leaving a review on the Amazon page. Have a great rest of the day.

Printed in Great Britain
by Amazon